Motivational & Inspirational Moments for Mental Wellness

#YourMentalHealthMatters!

Stephanie R. Booker, Licensed Professional Counselor

Acknowledgements:

I am beyond grateful to God for using me in the creation of this book. For over three years, I have sent "Monday Motivational Messages" to the people that I've worked with and been told how each one has poured into their lives.

A special thank you to Ralph (RIP) and Wayne Miller, who since I was in my twenties would ask me every time, they'd see me "Have you started on that book yet?" I finally started and finished it.

Thank you to my family, who encourages and supports me in everything I decide to do. You can never understand the magnitude of gratefulness that fills my heart, especially because ya'll know I stay with a plan.

All my love to each of you: Tony, William, Janice, Cynthia, Brandon, Brittnee, LaJarvia, Niesha, Anthony, Dahlia, Brianna, Montraill, Zayla, Paris, Brielle, Sean-Anthony, Dallas, Calvin, Coby, Karter, Karson, Kru, NaZaria, Anthony III, Au'Brielle & "Chicken Nugget."

Let's Get Started

It's often said that it's the *little* things that mean the most. So, take a mindful moment today to give;

A *little* extra time for someone having a rough day.

A *little* grace to the one that challenges you the most.

A *little* kindness to a stranger.

A *little* moment to yourself to just do NOTHING but take in the moment.

Because the **"little"** things can make a big difference in the life of someone else.

Moment of Reflection: Did you do any of these things? _____

Which one/ones? _____

_____

_____

How did it make you feel?

_____

_____

_____

How do you think it made the other person feel?

_____

_____

Notes:

As you begin this day, you may find yourself focused on and consumed with "*Stuff.*" There will be "**stuff**" that you need to do, **"Stuff"** you want to do, **"Stuff"** you wish you were able to do, but make sure that you take a moment for **YOU**. If you don't take care of you, none of that "**Stuff**" will matter. You cannot pour into someone else when you are on empty. You can't be effective when you are depleted. Remember that not only is it okay to sometimes put you first, but it's a necessity! #YourMentalHealthMatters!

What can I do for me today?

_____
_____
_____
_____

What did I do for me today?

_____
_____
_____

Notes:

Even in this gloomy weather, you should be intentional about letting your light shine. We used to hear people say, "When you look good, you feel good." A smile is an accessory that costs you nothing, yet it is worth a million bucks. So be intentional about smiling, it will make you feel better, and it has the power to brighten someone else's day. #YourMentalHealthMatters

Today, I will smile because…

_____
_____
_____

Matthew 5:14-15 (NIV)You are the light of the world. A town built on a hill cannot be hidden. Neither do people light a lamp and put it under a bowl. Instead they put it on its stand, and gives light to everyone in the house

Notes:

"Quitters never win, and winners never quit." Now be mindful that being a winner does not mean you won't get tired or that you won't have to make a pit stop or two (cause life be lif'in'). You may need to stretch, catch your breath, hydrate, or refuel, but it does mean that you **keep going** until you make it to the finish line **without** quitting. No matter how long it takes, you keep running the race!

In a steeplechase event, the runners run 3000 meters/1.86 miles, with 28 fixed barriers, including 7 water pits, and some hurdles. No matter who finishes ahead of them, every runner makes it to the finish line and the crowd keeps cheering until the race has ended.

Today, I wanted to quit _____, but I didn't because_____
_____
_____

Today, I declare that I am a winner! _____
Signature

Notes:

Learn to create boundaries and respect the boundaries you create because if you don't respect them, neither will other people! Remember that your mental health should always be a non-negotiable.

What boundaries have you created that are non-negotiable?

_____
_____
_____
_____
_____

What boundaries do you need to create and why? Understanding the "WHY" is important.

_____
_____
_____
_____
_____
_____
_____

Notes:

You've set goals and made plans for advancement or change in your life, whether it be personal, professional, mental, or spiritual, yet you haven't taken one step in making it happen. Stop operating in fear. Stop being complacent in your unhappiness, or your comfort zone becomes it provides familiarity. #YourMentalHealthMatters!

James 2:17 tells us that faith without works is dead. This means that there is some action required on your part for you to accomplish the plans and goals you have for yourself.

What goals have I set for myself that I have not begun to take steps to implement them, making them a reality?

_____
_____
_____
_____
_____

Notes:

Being surrounded means that you are being watched but being supported means that you are being helped. Be sure that you are surrounding yourself with people who **support** you and not just there to **watch** you. Those there to only watch, are awaiting your downfall, and not your accomplishments. Check your circle! #YourMentalHealthMatters!

Who are the people I can depend on in my life?
_____
_____
_____
_____

Whose presence do I need to re-evaluate and why?
_____
_____
_____
_____

Notes:

The word ==asset== is defined as a benefit, a blessing, adding something positive.

a ==*liability*== is defined as a hindrance, a burden, a stumbling block.

You sometimes have more impact on people than their own relatives, so be intentional about being an **asset** and not a **liability** in the lives of those that you encounter.

Working with young people places you on the frontline of defense for building strong character in tomorrow's leaders.

#YourMentalHealthMatters

How can I be an asset and not a liability to those that I encounter on my job?

_____
_____
_____

How can I be an asset and not a liability to those that I encounter in my family?

_____
_____
_____

How can I be an asset and not a liability to my community?

Remember that being an asset isn't always something tangible, however; it's something positive that adds to the situation, environment or circumstances.

Notes:

Retrieved from Google 12/18/24

Hydration: the replacement of body fluids lost through sweating, exhaling, and eliminating waste.

Make sure that you stay hydrated physically, mentally, emotionally, and spiritually. When we don't properly hydrate our bodies, we become drained and sluggish. This applies to your mental, emotional, and spiritual well-being as well, so be sure to find and implement ways to rehydrate your mind, body and spirit. #YourMentalHealthMatters

In what areas of my life do I need hydration?
_____
_____
_____

What can I do to rehydrate mentally?
_____
_____
_____

What can I do to rehydrate emotionally?
_____
_____
_____

What can I do to rehydrate physically?

_____

_____

_____

What can I do to rehydrate spiritually?

_____

_____

_____

Notes:

> You cannot talk butterfly language with caterpillar people.

Life often throws us unexpected curve balls, some which we can dodge and some that knock the wind from us. When facing these situations, take a moment to reflect on previous knowledge gained, evaluate the big picture, not just that moment before deciding how to move and what should be the next step. Hasty decisions often result in more curve balls thrown your way. So firmly plant your feet, get a good grip on the bat and prepare to knock those curve balls out the park. *#YourMentalHealthMatters*

What are the curve balls in your life right now?
_____
_____
_____
_____

What do you need to do to knock that curve ball out of the park?
_____
_____
_____
_____

Notes:

Sometimes God will place you in an uncomfortable position in order for you to truly focus on what you need to do, moves you need to make, and people that you need to shake from your life. Diamonds require pressure to become the brightest.

#YourMentalHealthMatters

What do you need to do for your light to shine brightest?

_____
_____
_____
_____

Mathew 5:14 "You are the light of the world. A city set on a hill cannot be hidden." (NIV, Zondervan, 2017).

Notes:

Did you know that it can take 1-3 weeks for germination of a planted seed, or even months depending on the environmental conditions. Remember, like the tree, you won't instantly sprout, and sometimes you may feel over-watered and other times, you may feel as if you're in a drought, and not getting enough water. Environment is also key to proper growth and nourishment, but the good news is that YOU get to help set the environment (attitude/disposition). If you need a little water, or feel over-watered, let's get some support before drowning or drying up. You are NOT alone. #StrongFinishItWillBe! #YourMentalHealthMatter

How do I respond when I feel overwhelmed?
_____
_____

Who can I go to for support?
_____

What kind of support do I need?
_____
_____

Notes:

Never allow others to determine/define your value/worth (It was already done on the cross). Speak positively to and over yourself. Write down an affirmation and place it where you see it daily or multiple times throughout the day, set a goal for the day or week and make it happen. *#YourMentalHealthMatters!*

What's the affirmation that speaks to you?

_____
_____
_____
_____
_____

What goal did you set for yourself today/the week?

_____
_____
_____
_____

Notes:

Remember that you have been positioned on purpose, for a purpose, and with a purpose. Stay focused and don't allow people or things to distract you from that which you have been purposed to perform.

Are you questioning *your* purpose? _____
Are you doing what you have been purposed to do in your life, or operating in fear and uncertainty?

_____
_____
_____

Who or what are you allowing to distract you from your purpose?

_____
_____
_____
_____

Notes:

Take a moment to evaluate your worth. Once you recognize your value and worth, you will realize that you don't always have to wait for an invite for a seat at the table. You may very well have it within yourself the fortitude, skills, & knowledge to build your own table, alone, or with like-minded individuals. #StopSleepingOnYou!

This may be the table you're awaiting an invite to, they just keep showing it to you in its original form. *#YourMentalHealthMatters*

Retrieved from Google 12/15/24

Notes:

Let's talk about the word "No."

"No," is a complete sentence.

"No," does not always require an explanation.

"No," is self-care and not always selfish

"No," is sometimes necessary to preserve your mental health, to save friendships, relationships, and set boundaries for yourself and with others.

"No," can prevent you from overextending yourself when you really have nothing left to give or any reserve for yourself.

Know when to say "No," and be okay with it.

#YourMentalHealthMatters

To who or what do you need to say "No"?

_____
_____
_____
_____

Notes:

During those special occasions and festive events where food is in abundance, and with so many options to choose from, we find ourselves putting a little of this and a little of that onto our plate causing us to overload our plates; & then we're complaining about a stomachache or that we ate way too much, knowing full well that you could have left some stuff off your plate. This is the same thing with our life plate. So often people say, "My plate is full!" Today, take a moment to evaluate what's on your plate, and what YOU have the power to remove to alleviate the stomachache (stress/anxiety) in your body, and your life. Again, remember that your mental/emotional well-being impacts your physical well-being.

What can you take off your plate today?

_____

_____

What can you permanently remove from your plate physically, mentally/emotionally, professionally, or spiritually?

_____

_____

Is there too much on my plate?

RaisingArrows.NET

Retrieved from Google 12/15/24

Notes:

Sometimes people will take from you even when you think you have nothing left to give. However, when you are at your lowest, you may be seen as an asset or inspirations to someone else, so keep allowing your light to shine, even when you are low on fuel. A dim light is better than complete darkness.

Luke 8:16 *"No man, when he hath lighted a candle, covereth it with a vessel, or putteth it under a bed; but setteth it on a candlestick, that they which enter in may see the light" (KJV).*

Retrieved from Google 15/15/24

Notes:

Life is full of big relationships, ie.... parental, marital, work, spiritual, friendships, romantic, professional etc... but the one thing that they all have in common is that when people feel valued and appreciated, they want to give more than what's required to keep the relationship thriving. **But**, when felt unseen, unheard, unvalued, and unappreciated even giving the bare minimum can seem like a giant task. Take a moment to let someone know that you appreciate them and what they do. It may change the trajectory of the relationship.

Who do you need to let know that you appreciate them and what they contribute to the shared relationship? What can that look like?

_____

_____

Who do you need or want to feel appreciated by? What does that look like for you?

_____

_____

_____

Notes:

Retrieved from Google 12/15/24

It's important that you take time to cheer for yourself **out loud** and encourage yourself **out loud** because you may not hear it from anyone else. This doesn't mean that others are not cheering for you, it's just sometimes people are silent cheerleaders, and there are times when you need to **HEAR** the encouragement and support. So, yell it as loud as you need to hear it because your mental health really does matter!

Notes:

As one year comes to an end, or at the beginning of a new year, many people make it a priority to create a vision board, which is a great idea, but how about in this chaotic world of constant change, you take a moment to create a monthly or quarterly vision board? Place it where is it visible on a regular basis and big moment............

Now **identify** the necessary steps to get your vision "OFF" the board into reality. Goals are great and we often set our long-term goals but become disheartened or frustrated when we don't see them becoming reality. Try setting quarterly goals and checking them off as they happen. If they are not reached during that time, take a moment of reflection to identify what you did or did not do to make them happen. What do you need to adjust or change about the plan to reach the desired goal? Put it back on your next quarterly vision board, journal your necessary steps of completion, and get your vision "OFF" the board.

What is one short-term goal you have set for yourself?

_____
_____
_____

What's the first step in making that goal a reality?

_____
_____
_____

What is a long-term you have for yourself?

_____
_____
_____

Have you identified the process needed? _____

Have you started the process to making it a reality?
_____

What's the first thing you need to do?
_____
_____
_____

Retrieved from Google 2/15/24

Notes:

Stop leaning on things not created to support you. Sometimes you must adjust your posture to get the results that you desire.

Remember that when one part of your body is out of alignment, it throws off your entire balance.

When your mental health is out of alignment, your entire body is out of alignment. When your spiritual life is out of alignment, your entire body is out of alignment. Being out of alignment is painful, whether we're talking about one's physical, mental, or spiritual well-being. Take time to stretch and allow proper rest and recovery in all these areas.

As you are running the marathon of life, know that this path is filled with trap doors, and rugged mountains. Yet, you have stayed in the race, slapped band aids on some of your bumps and bruises, but it's only a temporary fix until take time to get back in alignment that you may be able to experience complete restoration.

Notes:

Whew Chile, exhale, and take a moment to reflect on the glows and grows of your last seven days. Celebrate your successes and give yourself **grace** as you smooth out the rough edges.

Remember that the race is not given to the swift, but to the one who endures to the end. So, let's tighten up our shoes and run this race!

What can you celebrate about you from the last 7 days? It doesn't have to be anything big, take time to celebrate even the small accomplishments.

_____
_____
_____
_____

What did you do or begin in the last days that didn't quite work out the way you planned, and you need to rethink, readjust or just scrap it?

_____
_____
_____

Notes:

Sometimes it seems as if obstacles (people, things, stuff) are placed in pathway to hinder your progress, disrupt your energy, or try your patience. Remember no matter how it makes you "FEEL," you still get to "CHOOSE" how you respond and react. Inhale! Exhale! Push through! You got this!

Who or what is an obstacle in your pathway?

_____
_____
_____
_____

What is the best way to deal with or handle the situation?

_____
_____
_____
_____

Notes:

Every challenge that you face is not always for you. Sometimes it's for others to see how YOU respond and react when faced with adversity so that they may grow and believe that they too are able to conquer and overcome. Remember that someone is always watching, so move with integrity.

#YourMentalHealthMatters

Reflect on a challenge you faced or that someone else faced, but someone else was strengthened, renewed, revived, or given hope.

_____
_____
_____
_____
_____

Notes:

Remember that being comfortable is not always a good thing because we can become complacent. It's when you step out of your comfort zone, shift into new opportunities, and exposure to new things that you may experience your biggest adventure, greatest accomplishment, or truly pursue your truest passion.

Don't be afraid to step out of your comfort zone. (Walk by faith).

#YourMentalHealthMatters #MyMentalHealthIsNonnegotiable

Am I allowing myself to be complacent in a situation, occupation because I'm afraid of change? What moves do I need to make?

_____

_____

_____

_____

_____

Notes:

Remember despite what it looks like, and the challenges that may be thrown your way, you were purposed for this moment. You can be the difference maker for every person that you encounter, so take a deep breath, remember who/whose you are, and what you have been called to do.

Have an amazing day!

Look in the mirror and remind yourself that you are built for "this". Whatever your "THIS" may be, you can and will handle it.

What is your "This?"

_____

_____

_____

_____

Notes:

Remember that your energy is contagious, so you decide if you want to be ground zero for light or for darkness! You get to *set or shift* the atmosphere in every environment you enter.

Retrieved from Google 12/15/25

What did you do today to *shift* the atmosphere instead of simply matching energy?

_____
_____
_____

Notes:

Life is filled with *loss and lessons*. With every **loss**, there is a **lesson**, and if you learn nothing from the **loss**, then you are definitely **lost**! Make sure you get the lesson! Have a great day, or not. The *choice* is yours!

Loss is defined as the fact or process of losing something or someone (Oxford Dictionary, 2024).

A *lesson* is defined as a situation in which you learn something useful (Oxford Dictionary, 2024).

Lost is defined as unable to find one's way; off track; disoriented (Oxford Dictionary, 2024).

What are some valuable lessons learned from a loss?

_____
_____
_____
_____
_____

Notes:

Be content in whatever season you are in, but don't allow your **contentment** to become **complacency** rendering you stuck just because you are **comfortable**.

#YourMentalHealthMatters!

Have I allowed myself to become complacent? _____

What should I do to move to the next stage in my life?
_____
_____
_____
_____

Notes:

In the fall, time goes back one hour and for one night, we were able to capture an additional hour of sleep. In the spring, time moves forward one hour, reclaiming that hour in the fall, and we lose one hour of sleep. However, the reality of life is that there are only 24 hours in a day, and time is the one true thing that you can never recapture. Take time to love on yourself and those who mean the most to you.

Who do I need to be intentional about showing love?
_____
_____
_____

Today, I will show myself love by
_____
_____
_____
_____

Notes:

Up until this very moment in your life, you have incurred some battles along the way, but based on the fact that you're still here, means that you won. Take a break to celebrate you. You deserve some "Me" time, some family time, some relaxing time, and simply some time off to rest and reset.

How can you celebrate you?
_____
_____
_____
_____

What does "Me" time look like for you?
_____
_____
_____
_____

Notes:

We always say, "You can't pour from an empty cup." However, there are times that we must examine what's in our cups. Today, take a moment to examine the contents of your cup, and see if it's time to give your cup a good washing before you refill it.

What's in your cup that may need to be washed out? (hate, envy, jealousy, lack of confidence etc...)

_____
_____
_____
_____

Notes:

Stop carrying bags (physical, mental, emotional, spiritual, & people) that weigh you down. Some weight we carry is a choice. That being said, take some time to self-evaluate and self-reflect on the excess baggage in your life that's weighing you down. Next, formulate a plan to lighten your load. Your mental health could depend on it. #YourMentalHealthMatters!

What bags are weighing you down?
_____
_____
_____

What do you need to lighten your load? Make a plan.
_____
_____
_____
_____

Getty pictures (Google, 2024)

Notes:

We will have to deal with accidents, incidents, and inconveniences throughout this lifetime. Assess what you can control, what's out of your control, and then remember that God is forever in control. So, take a moment to pause, pray, and push through. You got this, whatever your "THIS" may be.

#YourMentalHealthMatters

What things can I control?

_____
_____
_____
_____

What is out of my control?

_____
_____
_____
_____

What is my prayer for the situation in which I lack control?

_____
_____
_____

Notes:

Today, take about 15 seconds to simply inhale and exhale. It doesn't have to be deep breathing, just breathe and focus on your breath, and on your heartbeat. Both are a precious commodity that someone loss the privilege of on this very day.

Wednesday is referenced as "Hump" day. When we are on the hump, it means that we have reached the middle, giving us a glimpse of what we made it through, and a glimpse of what we need to make it to. When you get to the "**Hump"** in your day, focus on your breath/heartbeat and have a day of hakuna matata. You are worth it, and you deserve it!

What did I accomplish by the middle of my day?
_____
_____
_____

I will commit to taking time to simply focus on my breathing for at least 15 seconds today. _____ (Initial on the line).

Notes:

If you feel worn down after a full day's work, that means you have put in the work. Now, when you clock out today, rest, reset and get sharp once again because it's hard to work with a dull pencil the entire day.

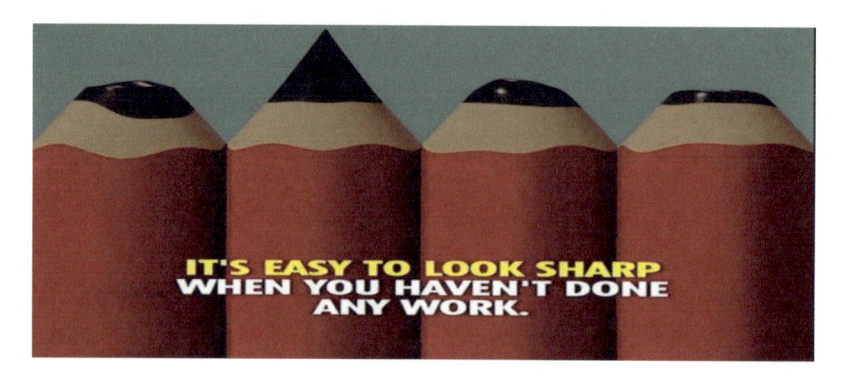

Retrieved from Google, 2024)

What were your glows and grows for the day?

Glows:

_____

_____

Grows:

_____

_____

Notes:

In life we have to learn to pivot when faced with unexpected situations and circumstances. Frustrations will come, and although you lack control over what has already happened.... ie...busted water pipes, flooded classrooms, freezing weather, or inconsiderate individuals, you most certainly control how you respond and react. Remember that the way in which you respond and react can not only impact your physical health (headache, stomachache, blood pressure, etc..), but it can also affect your work productivity and effectiveness, as well as your mental and emotional well-being. So, learn to pivot and do it with grace. In this world of education, you are the "Sunshine" that provides energy to the ones you encounter. #YourMentalHealthMatters

What life situations has required you to pivot from the path you set for yourself? What positive came from the unexpected pivot?

_____

_____

_____

_____

_____

Notes:

Having an attitude of gratitude is not always easy, but that's because it is one of intentionality. You have to take a moment to reflect on the things you are or should be grateful for. You may have woken up on this Monday morning feeling like "Ugh! I really hate that I have to work this morning." When you should be grateful for the job. Somebody is on a search, not because they want to be, but because they were released from their job. You had to *decide* what you wanted to wear today. This wasn't an option for everyone. I could go on and on, but you get the picture, so for your moment of self-care today, take 3-5 minutes to reflect on what & who you are grateful for in your life and then demonstrate an attitude of gratitude throughout your day.

That means because you are grateful for your job, you are going to give 100% in all that you do. That person you are grateful for but haven't spoken to in a minute because life be "lifen'," give them a call and let them know. This could very well change the trajectory of their day as well.

What are you grateful for today and at this point in your life?

_____

_____

_____

Notes:

_____

_____

_____

_____

_____

_____

_____

_____

_____

_____

_____

_____

_____

_____

Retrieved from Google 12/15/24

Don't be so focused on reaching the mountain top that you miss the benefits and blessings in the valley. Your mountain top can be personal or professional goals and ambitions. The valley is where you encounter friends, clients, contacts, contracts, connections, lessons, skills, knowledge and provisions to use once you reach the mountain top, and you just may need assistance to carry all that you need to the top, so move with integrity.

#YourMentalHealthMatters

What's your mountain top(s)?

_____

_____

Who or what is your valley blessings?

_____

_____

What actions have you made that may be blocking your mountain top journey?

_____

_____

Notes:

Change is inevitable, and growth is a choice. You get make a choice on whether you will remain stagnant in the situation or circumstances that you find undesirable, or if you will learn and grow from those experiences and move forward. Your mental health may depend on it. #YourMentalHealthMatters!

In what areas in your life do you need to be intentional about making growth?
_____
_____
_____

What does that growth look like?
_____
_____
_____

Notes:

A Moment of Physical Decompression

Mental health awareness includes taking time for self-evaluation. Often times we over-internalize situations and circumstances, but never truly process them, which in turn creates stress and anxiety. One thing I always say is "Not enough commas, not enough zeros to stress me out." However true it may be, sometimes I feel tightness in my shoulders, which is my body's response to stress. Be conscious of how your body responds to stress and take a purposeful moment to decompress. *#YourMentalHealthMatters!*

Take about 5 minutes to do a self-mental health check, and stress release.

Follow these steps

Sit in a quiet place, in a chair with your feet flat.

Place your hands flat on your lap. You will close your eyes, lean your head all the way to the left as far as you can.

Take a deep breath in through your nose (Lift/pull your shoulders back with the inhale). Slowly release the breath and your shoulders. Complete this step 5 times.

Tilt your head forward & repeat the breathing process.

Tilt your head to the right & repeat.

Tilt your head all the way back & repeat.

Arms hanging at your sides and do a little shake.

Take notice of how you & your body felt before and after.

Notes:

Don't allow your disappointments in people, situations, or circumstances deter you from what you have been called to do. The mask was removed for you to see who the person really is. The situation and circumstances shifted to make it better for you, even when you didn't see it that way. Stay the course, even when you have been disappointed by life, because life stay lif'in'.

What disappointments have caused you to make a detour from what you know you are supposed to do?

_____
_____
_____

What do you need to do to get back on track?

_____
_____
_____

Notes:

If you are anything like me, 23 of your 24 hours in the day are consumed with things to do. You haven't seen 8hrs of sleep since forever, and everybody is tugging you in one direction or another. Now with all of that being said, you must remember that self-care is not a treat, but a necessity. We all too often find ourselves simply operating off of fumes, but just like a car that has run out of gas, the fumes will only get you so far before it conks out. Take five minutes of **this** day to simply ground yourself. Close your eyes, think about something or someone who brings joy to your life, take a deep breath and slowly exhale. Tell yourself "I got this!" Set yourself a self-care goal for this month, write it down and then hold yourself accountable. Whatever your "THIS" is, remember, you got **this**!

Who or what is it that brings you joy?

_____
_____
_____

What reasonable/attainable goal can you set for *this* month?

_____
_____
_____

Notes:

When a car accident occurs, the car is not just assessed and appraised on the external damage. They have to look beneath the surface to see what internal parts have been affected and sustained damage. Although we look good on the outside, we must take time to assess and appraise our internal damage (mental, emotional, and spiritual) because life be lif'in' causing us some external hits. Assess yourself before you have a meltdown or blow-up and find yourself out for extended repair!! #YourMentalHealthMatters

What external hits have cause you internal damage?

_____
_____
_____

Have you taken time to truly assess the damage?

_____

What will it take for the repairs?

_____
_____
_____

Notes:

We always say that we need to refuel or get refilled, but what are you refueling/refilling with? If you put diesel fuel in your car and it isn't made for diesel, it will clog the fuel filters and injectors, mess up the spark plugs, and damage your engine. Just like it's important to PROPERLY fuel your car to prevent stalling, damage, or breakdown when you need it to go, you have to properly fuel your mind, body and spirit to allow you to function in a healthy and positive manner. Take a moment of positive self-talk and determine what you need for proper refueling/refilling for the day/week. Remember that repairs usually cost more than proper maintenance.

#YourMentalHealthMatters!

Notes:

We are most times harder on ourselves than anyone else could ever be. To others, it may not always seem like you are making a difference, showing growth or progress, but no-one sees what's going on in the cocoon, they just see the butterfly that emerges. Allow yourself grace to complete all the necessary steps in your growth journey.

What growth are you most proud about?

_____
_____
_____

What area do you need more time to develop?

_____
_____
_____

What areas do your NEED help?

_____
_____
_____

Notes:

Stop holding yourself hostage in places you're not intended to be! Your mental and physical health may be dependent on it.

In what things and places are you allowing yourself to be held hostage?
_____
_____
_____

How is it affecting your life?
_____
_____
_____

What do you need to do to be released?
_____
_____
_____

Notes:

Sometimes in our lives, we find ourselves personally or professionally frustrated and ready to respond and react in a not so nice manner. However, our character is what we are known for and by, so when faced with those challenges, take a moment to decide if that person or situation is really worth stepping outside of your character. Contrary to what some may think, an apology doesn't erase the action, nor does it make the person forget what was said or done. *Stay true to yourself!*

Who or what situations made me want to come out of character today/this week/this month?

_____
_____
_____

How did you handle it?

_____
_____
_____

Could you have handled it better? _____
How so?

_____
_____
_____

On every obituary, there is the date of birth, "dash," and the date of death. Remember that the dash represents your character.

What will your dash say about you?

_____
_____
_____
_____

What do you want it to say?

_____
_____
_____
_____

What do you need to do to change it?

_____
_____
_____
_____

Notes:

Retrieved from Google 12/15/24

For My Educators

In a relay race, the runner passes off the baton, then the next runner gives it all they have to get to the next person. As an educator, YOU are the runner, and the students are the batons. Our batons have been dropped many times and some have now gotten behind in the race, but **YOU** have the opportunity to make up some of the distance lost as you prepare to pass the baton to the next runner. Don't give up and hold the baton firmly because right now it's in your hands. You must have the mindset of an Olympian, and never give-up, even when your baton is chipped, discolored, or a little slippery. #YouAreTheDifferenceMaker!

Who are your challenging batons, and what do you need to hold on a little tighter to keep from losing your grip?

_____
_____
_____
_____
_____

Notes:

When I do group sessions with incarcerated clients, or recently released clients who are required to do group counseling, one of the things I ask is that they share one "positive" thing about their incarceration. So many times, the answer is the same with individuals stating that incarceration saved their life, because they would have kept doing whatever they were doing that rendered them incarcerated.

Finding the positive in every situation is not always the easiest thing to do, but when you are intentional about doing so, it helps to have an attitude of gratitude despite the situation or circumstances. Never say you had a bad day. You had some bad moments in your day.

Changing your mindset is essential to changing your outlook!
#YourMentalHealthMatters!

What were your bad moments in your day?

_____
_____
_____

Now, what were the positives in those bad moments?

_____
_____
_____

Notes:

Retrieved from Google 12/15/24 ICanvas

Life is not a sprint, but a marathon filled with mazes, obstacles, and pitfalls that we must face, maneuver, and overcome. Everyone doesn't require the same level of conditioning and workout to run the race. Remember that you may not be able to climb the tall wall, but you can stack crates/blocks to get you over. You may not be able to swim across the water, but you can use a boat, or even jet skis. You have to take time to identify what *you* need to finish the race, how you need to maneuver the obstacles, and the that includes what's needed mentally, emotionally, and spiritually to endure all that you are faced with at this point in your race (life). *#YourMentalHealthMatters!*

What obstacles/mazes/pitfalls are you facing in this marathon of life?

_____
_____
_____

What are some necessities to help you move beyond these "temporary barriers?"

_____
_____
_____

What is your plan to move past these "temporary barriers," and get you moving toward the finish line?

_____

_____

_____

Notes:

You can't expect a harvest when you haven't planted **any** seeds.

Now, you must also remember that you can **only** produce what you have planted, so if you plant negative thoughts/emotions that's what you will grow. Be intentional about what you plant in your mental, emotional, spiritual well-being because that's exactly what you will harvest. *#YourMentalHealthMatters!*

Are you looking for a harvest (results)personal, professional or spiritually, but haven't planted any seeds (made steps to make it happen)?

_____

_____

_____

What harvest are you seeking in your relationships, but either you have planted no seeds, failed to water the seeds, or allowed weeds (bad choices, people, etc…) to damage your harvest?

_____

_____

_____

Notes:

If you buy a new house, the old keys won't allow you entry, nor will your old keys operate your new car. You can't always use the same tools to operate in new spaces, so don't be afraid of change as it is often needed for growth and elevation. I love butterflies, but in order for it to spread its beautiful wings and fly, it had to endure some changes. Although if you truly examine it, it still has the body of a caterpillar, but now it's reaching heights and going places, it was forbidden to explore before change occurred in its life. Learn to embrace the new.
#YourMentalHealthMatters!

What new ventures are you trying to enter, but you still have the same old mindset?

_____
_____
_____

What do you need to change (attitude, company kept, career, level of faith)?

_____
_____
_____

Notes:

Stop settling or limiting yourself to the **group** when you have been called and assigned to **the masses**. It's time to self-examine to determine what's holding you hostage from your growth and destination.

It's time for you to exercise your faith, believe in yourself, and stop depriving the world of your greatness. Stop believing that you are only good enough to be the opening act, when God intended for you to be the main event AND the main finale.

What areas of your life have you set limits when you know you should be doing more?

_____

_____

_____

What's needed in order for you to do or be more than what you are allowing yourself to settle for?

_____

_____

_____

Notes:

During times when the weather becomes unbearably cold, it may require you to put on some extra layers of clothing to combat the elements. This is the same way with life. You may face situations where you find yourself in a struggle mentally, emotionally, spiritually, personally, or professionally where you may need to put on some extra layers to push you through the elements. Now, determine what are the extra layers that **YOU** need. Do you already possess these layers or do you need assistance in securing them, ie counseling, prayer life, social/professional connect ect... In other words, do you have a plan & the essentials you need to work the plan?

What are the extra layers needed by you?

_____
_____
_____

Where can you get the needed layers?

_____
_____
_____

Notes:

It's possible to make a comeback when you are focused on the assignment (what you have been purposed to do), and not the assassin (your haters and nay sayers). Reflect on the fact that you have made it this far, and yes you have incurred some bumps and bruises along the way, BUT, yet you have made it. Take a moment to celebrate the triumphs, and not the "could of", "should of", "would of" moments. Remember to ask yourself "What part do I control? If you don't control it, move through it with integrity and grace.

What's my assignment?

_____
_____
_____

Who or what are my assassins? What does that look like?

_____
_____
_____

What are my actions needed to refocus?

_____
_____
_____

What can I celebrate?

_____
_____
_____

Notes:

_____
_____
_____
_____
_____
_____
_____
_____
_____
_____
_____
_____
_____
_____
_____

For those in Leadership

When in a position of leadership, you must be cognizant that no matter what you do, everyone on your team won't follow the path set. Some people are in position to enhance your leadership skills by presenting challenges, and dilemmas for you to manage with style, grace, and professionalism, creating opportunities for others to see the true abilities and character of an effective leader. Don't stress, don't get frustrated, but get creative. Remember that your mental health effects/affects your physical well-being, and your leadership can affect/effect the mental health of those that you lead. #LeadwithIntegrity.

What does my leadership say about my character?
_____
_____
_____

Does it align with what I desire it to reflect?
_____

What can I do different to better enhance my leadership style?
_____
_____

Who are the one that challenge me the most?

_____

_____

_____

Why do I feel challenged by them?

_____

_____

_____

Integrity: A Crucial Foundation for Effective Leadership

Retrieved from Google 12/15/24

Notes:

You should decide to enter into this next chapter of your life with a mindset to make a positive impact on everyone that you encounter. be intentional about loving you, relax more, reward yourself for the little things, and celebrate you, simply because you're worth it.

What is it that I desire for this chapter of my life?
_____
_____
_____

What can I do to intentionally show love for myself?
_____
_____
_____

What activities can I do to relax and how often will I do so?
_____
_____
_____

What have I done today, this week, and this month that I can celebrate?
_____
_____
_____

Notes:

Some people will do things to challenge your character simply because they don't like you, can't compete with you, or they may even be envious or jealous of you and your life. Don't get mad about it, as it really is a compliment to you in the most *unflattering* way. Keep moving in integrity, you're doing something right.

Who are the people that attempt to challenge my character most?

_____

_____

_____

Notes:

Everything ain't to be shared with everyone. Some people just want to know your game plan so they know how and where to place obstacles. Before you start speaking, evaluate the environment & determine if you need be like the "G" in lasagna in order to guard your peace.

What are some things you wished that you had moved in silence about?
_____
_____
_____

I need to move in silence about?
_____
_____
_____

Notes:

If you have ever watched the tv show McGiver, then you know no matter what situation he was faced, he'd find and use things to enable him to safely escape and survive. You need to have a McGiver mentality and use what you have to make it work for your good instead of waiting for others to create opportunities for your win in life. In the wise words of Dori, "Just Keep swimming."

What am I facing right now that requires a McGiver and Dori mentality?

_____

_____

_____

What resources have I overlooked that can be an asset to me?

_____

_____

_____

Notes:

Lastly, I leave with you my personal motto. "Remember that every stumbling block is merely a steppingstone on your pathway to success". There are times that we are going to stumble, and maybe even fall, but we take those things that tripped us up, and we use them to elevate us to the next level. In other words, use what tripped you up to lift you up. No losses, only lessons!
#YourMentalHealthMatters!

What stumbling blocks (situations, circumstances, and life events) have tripped you up, but you have learned from them, and can now be elevated because of those "stumbling blocks?"

_____
_____
_____

Notes:

I pray that this book has been an asset to your life. Please feel free to provide me your feedback @ stephbooker731@gmail.com

Stephanie Booker, M.Ed., LPC, LSOTP

Licensed Professional Counselor

Owner: Better Days Therapy & Wellness

Made in the USA
Columbia, SC
30 January 2025